Girls Got Game

girls' ICE HOCKEY

Dominating the Rink

by Tami Johnson

Consultant
Yevet Anderson
Erie Lady Lions Girls Hockey
USA Hockey Master Level Coach

Capstone press®

Mankato, Minnesota

Snap Books are published by Capstone Press,
151 Good Counsel Drive, P.O. Box 669, Mankato, Minnesota 56002.
www.capstonepress.com

Library of Congress Cataloging-in-Publication Data

Johnson, Tami.
 Girls' ice hockey: dominating the rink / by Tami Johnson.
 p. cm.—(Snap books. Girls got game)
 Summary: "Describes girls' ice hockey, including positions, leagues, and
famous professionals in the sport"—Provided by publisher.
 Includes bibliographical references and index.
 ISBN-13: 978-1-4296-0133-7 (hardcover)
 ISBN-10: 1-4296-0133-7 (hardcover)
 1. Hockey for girls—Juvenile literature. 2. Hockey for women—
Juvenile literature. 3. Women hockey players—Juvenile literature. I. Title.
II. Series.
GV848.6.W65J65 2008
796.962082—dc22   2007002483

Editors: Kendra Christensen and Jennifer Besel

Designer: Bobbi J. Wyss

Photo Researchers: Charlene Deyle and Scott Thoms

Photo Credits:
AP/Wide World Photos/Denis Paquin, 27; Ed Andrieski, 28; Jonas Ekstromer, 21; Veli-Matti Parkkinen, 5, 24–25
Capstone Press/Karon Dubke, 9, 10–11, 12, 15, 17, 23
Comstock, Inc., back cover, 8
Corbis/David Stoecklein, 18–19; Reuters/Petr Josek, cover; Wally McNamee, 7
Getty Images Inc./Staff/Jim McIsaac, 26, 29
National Archives of Canada/Charlotte Whitton Collection, 6
Tami Johnson, 32

**Capstone Press thanks the Minnesota State University, Mankato, Women's Ice Hockey Team and
All Seasons Arena in Mankato, Minnesota, for their assistance with this book.**

The publisher does not endorse products whose logos may appear on objects in images in this book.

1 2 3 4 5 6 12 11 10 09 08 07

TABLE OF CONTENTS

CHAPTER ONE

BURYING THE BISCUIT

Imagine rushing across the ice controlling a small, round puck with a wooden stick. Suddenly, a defensive player skates toward you, determined to steal the puck.

You look up, see the goalie, and notice one small, unguarded corner. You shoot and bury that biscuit in the back of the net. Score!

Right now, it might be just in your imagination, but with a lot of hard work you can turn your dream of becoming a star hockey player into reality.

Girls play hockey for many reasons. Some players have Olympic dreams, while others just want to have fun. Whether you are super competitive or just out for some exercise, girls' hockey is one way-cool sport.

Anna-Kaisa
Piiroinen
(Finland Goalie)

Girls Got Gusto

Women have been playing hockey for more than 100 years. And they haven't just filled in when a men's team was short a player. In 1894, a women's hockey team formed at Queen's University in Kingston, Ontario. Another Canadian women's hockey team, the Rivulettes, earned a stunning 348–2 win-loss record in the 1930s.

In 1927, goalie Elizabeth Graham started wearing a wire mask to protect her face. That was more than 30 years before Jacques Plante, the National Hockey League player who first wore a goalie mask on November 2, 1959.

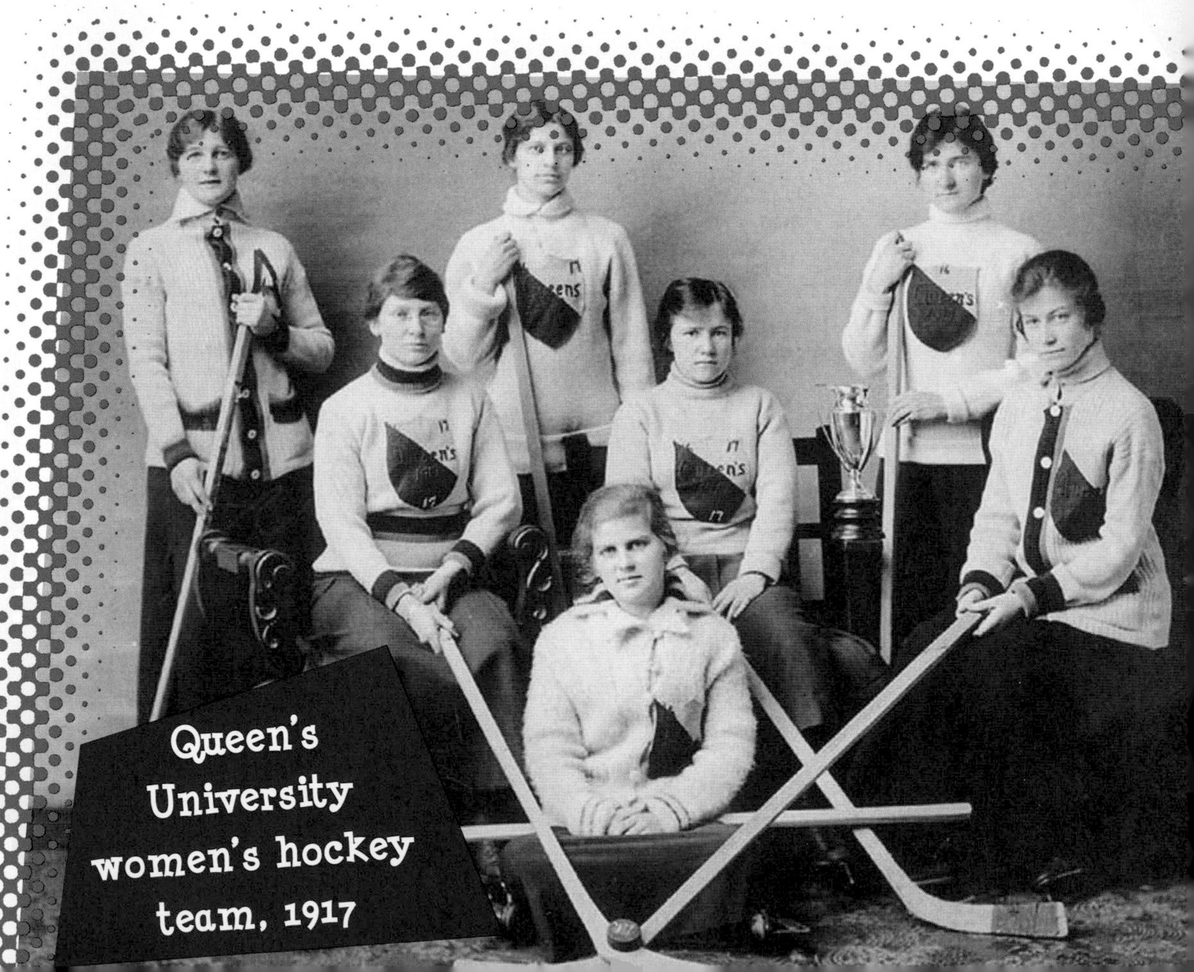

Queen's University women's hockey team, 1917

1998 USA
Olympic Team

Only recently has women's hockey found the respect and attention it deserves. Women's ice hockey made its Olympic debut in 1998 at the Winter Olympics in Nagano, Japan. The U.S. Women's team fought hard and played smart to defeat the Canadian team and bring home the gold.

Everything Goes with Black and Blue

Elite hockey players are among the best-conditioned athletes in the world. Girls rock at hockey because they use speed, strength, and stick handling skills instead of hitting opponents, or body checking. Does that mean girls can't be aggressive playing hockey? No way!

Women's hockey might not have body checking, but there is plenty of body contact. Make no bones about it—hockey is physical. You're going to fall on the ice. You may run into the boards or another player.

Bumps and bruises come with the territory. That's why players wear helmets and protective equipment. But all that equipment is a bonus in disguise. Your equipment bag may be big and heavy, but just think of it as extra strength training!

What's in that Equipment Bag?

Hockey is an aggressive sport. Besides your skates and your stick, you'll need to have the right equipment that will keep you from getting all banged up.

Helmets, gloves, elbow and shin pads, and shoulder pads are a great start. But you'll also need padded shorts called breezers, socks, and a mouth guard. Now do you see why that bag gets so heavy?

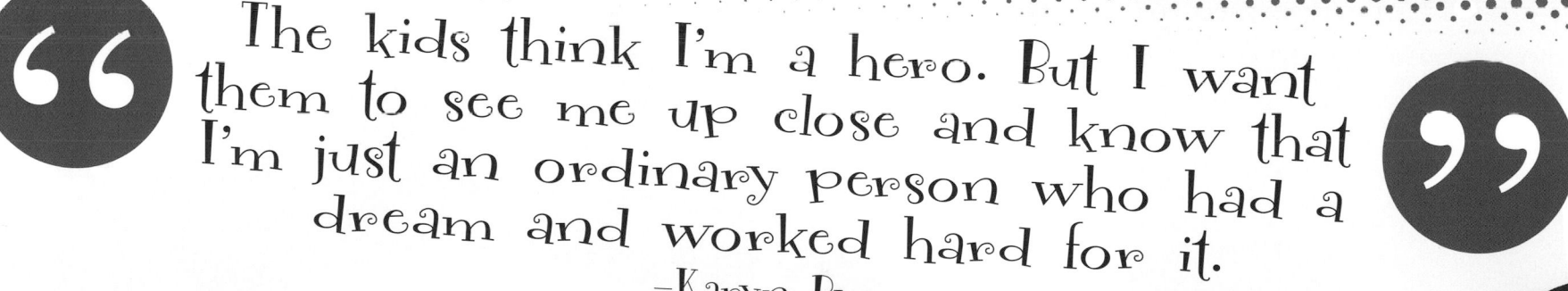

“ The kids think I'm a hero. But I want them to see me up close and know that I'm just an ordinary person who had a dream and worked hard for it. ”

-Karyn Bye
Women's Ice Hockey Olympian and five-time member of the U.S. Women's National Team

CHAPTER TWO

STICKING TO THE RULES

The object of hockey is simple—get the puck into the opponent's net. But getting it there isn't quite as simple. You can't kick the puck into the net. You can't bat it in with your glove, either.

When a player breaks the rules, the ref stops play. Play starts again with a face-off. But breaking some rules doesn't just stop the game. Trip a player and you'll get two minutes in the penalty box. This "time out" is no joke. Your team will play without you while you're in the box.

So learn the rules, stick by them, and you already have an advantage on the ice.

What Will Land You In the Box

While there are a number of penalties that can land you in the box, these are the most common. Remember to always play fair and with good sportsmanship. That will keep you out of the box and on the ice.

- **body checking**–using your body to push an opponent and make her lose possession of the puck

- **hooking**–using your stick to tug or pull on any part of an opponent's body

- **slashing**–swinging your stick at an opponent's body or stick (whether or not you make contact)

- **high sticking**–carrying the stick above the shoulders to use against an opponent

- **tripping**–just like it sounds, using a stick, arm, or leg to cause an opponent to trip or fall

What Position Is Right for You?

Each team starts a hockey game with five skaters and one goalie. Every player has a special responsibility on the ice. The goalie's job is to keep the puck out of the net. The two defensive players have to stop opponents from getting off quality shots on their goal. The three offensive players have the big job of getting that puck in the net. But if the puck is in your zone, everyone has to defend.

Goalie

The puck stops here. Goalies must be fearless, fast, and focused. The goalie stands alone. She is often considered the most important player on the ice.

Center

The center must be the leader and set up the play. You'll be facing your opponent where the puck is dropped. You'll need quick reactions to get control of the puck and pass it to your teammates.

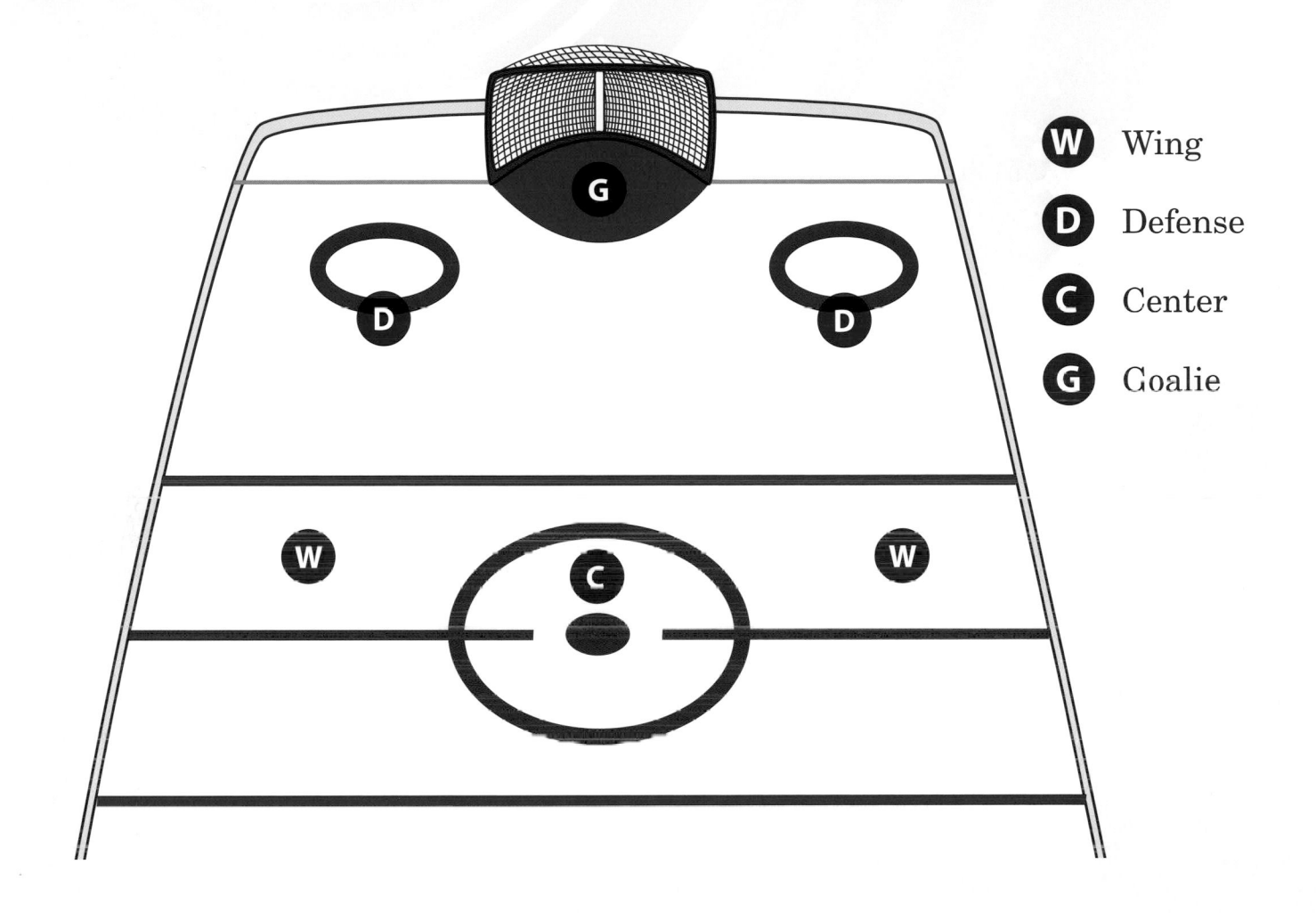

W Wing

D Defense

C Center

G Goalie

Wing

Good at puck handling? Fast on your skates? Love to shoot the puck? Wings are offensive players who most often score goals.

Defense

Defensive skaters do their best to stop the other team from scoring. They try to knock the puck off the opponent's stick or cut off their passing lanes.

CHAPTER THREE

JOINING THE TEAM

Learning to skate properly is the first step to becoming a hockey player. Lessons might be a good idea. But the best way to be a better skater is to practice. Remember, every time you get off the ice you're a better skater than you were when you got on.

The next step is to find a team to play with. Check out your local ice arena. Look for flyers or posters on the bulletin board. Ask the arena staff about girls' hockey programs in your area. Most youth hockey associations have Web sites with information on how to join.

If you live in a cold-weather climate, there's bound to be some frozen rink, pond, or lake somewhere outdoors. Where there's ice, there are bound to be skaters. Ask around. Find out who else likes to play hockey. Even a game at the park is a good place to start.

" I learned to stick handle at the outdoor rinks. I would go down there for hours during the day with my brother and our teammates and just stick handle around and even sometimes play tennis ball hockey. "
—Krissy Wendell,
U.S. Olympian and member of the U.S. Women's National Team

Practice Makes Perfect

The goal of all your hard work and practice is a place on a hockey team. But once you're on a team, practice is more important than ever. Your coach will hold regular practices with the team. It's important for you and the rest of your teammates to show up on time for every practice.

Serious hockey players will look for even more opportunities to practice. Hockey clinics and camps are a great way to improve your game. You'll work on skills like shooting, stick handling, passing, and power skating.

Hockey clinics can last a single day, a weekend, or even an entire week. For most clinics, you'll go home each night and sleep in your own bed. But at hockey camp, you'll pack your bags and stay at camp for a week or more. You'll live, eat, sleep, and play hockey with other girls you've never met before. It's a great way to make new friends and become a better hockey player.

Training at Home

You can work on some of your hockey skills right at home. You won't need skates or ice to practice stick handling in your basement or driveway. Practice moving a training puck or tennis ball back and forth with your hockey stick. Don't slap or chop at the ball. Keep your top hand firm on the stick and your bottom hand loose. Practice stick handling 15 to 20 minutes at a time, three to four times a week.

Rec and Travel Leagues

Leagues are groups of teams who compete against each other. Most leagues are separated into divisions according to skill level.

Recreational leagues are generally low-key and aimed at fun and friendly competition. Rec leagues offer players the opportunity to develop skills in locally based programs. In these leagues, the competition may be less intense but the fun level is sky high!

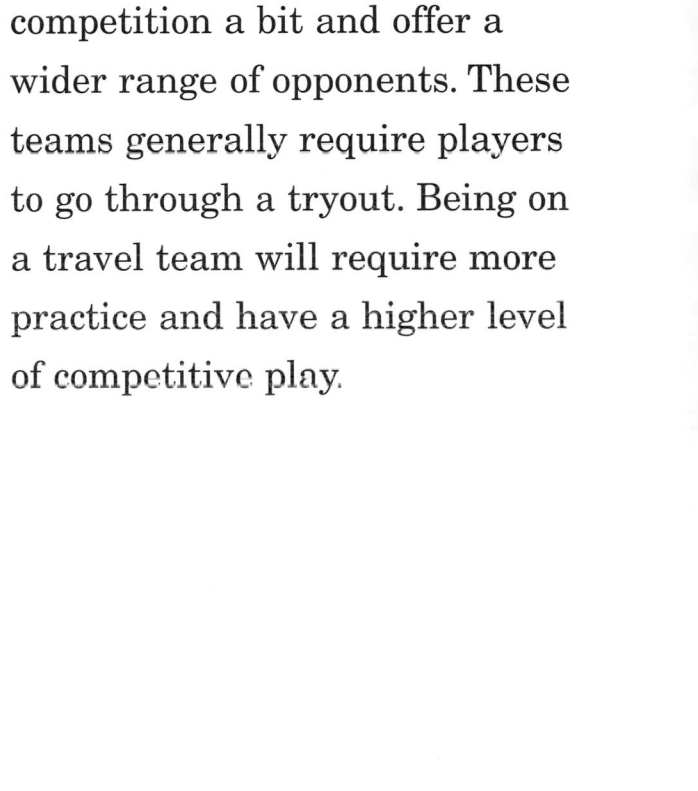

Travel leagues step up the competition a bit and offer a wider range of opponents. These teams generally require players to go through a tryout. Being on a travel team will require more practice and have a higher level of competitive play.

High School and College Play

High school and college hockey is another rung up on the competitive ladder. It requires serious skill and devotion to play on the varsity team. Junior varsity and smaller teams allow players to compete at a less intense level of play.

Like travel leagues, you have to tryout to make the high school team. Equipment like jerseys, helmets, breezers, and travel expenses may be provided by your school or booster club.

If you've got what it takes to play college hockey, exposure is key. College scouts watch high school and travel league games, looking for girls they might want on their teams. Tournaments and camps are also a great place for players to get noticed by recruiters. That's why you want to play your best every time. You never know who's in the stands watching.

Highly skilled and dedicated girls may go on to National and Olympic teams to fulfill their hockey dreams.

Making the Grade

What do As and Bs have to do with hockey? Quite a bit if you want to go on to play college hockey. High school grades are as important as hockey skills if you want a college scholarship. If you can't make the grade, you can't play hockey in college.

CHAPTER FOUR

BEING THE BEST

The best players really know the game. They have a sixth sense about where the puck is and can anticipate where it is going next. The best hockey players aren't afraid to miss. They make as many shots on the goal as they can. They never stop trying.

Speed, stick handling, and stamina are what make hockey players champions. Speed speaks for itself. Stick handling requires "soft hands" that can control the puck. And stamina is staying power—you can't give up or wear out.

A player's size doesn't really matter. The other team may have players who are taller, stronger, or faster. That doesn't mean they're better. Believe in yourself, listen to your coach, do your best, and you can become a champion.

A Sport for Life

Will you ever be one of the elite players who makes the women's Olympic hockey team? Anything is possible! But you don't have to be an Olympian to keep playing hockey. The number of recreational leagues and tournaments grows each year. Chances are, you'll have the opportunity to play hockey as long as you are able to skate.

What does hockey have to offer beyond great cardio endurance and muscular strength? How about flexibility, coordination, balance, and speed?

Caroline Ouellette (Canada)

And remember, hockey is about more than physical fitness. Being part of a competitive team can contribute a lot to mental and emotional health. Hockey helps you maintain overall fitness for life.

CHAPTER FIVE

PRO PLAYERS

Pioneers in women's hockey played the game when many people didn't think girls should. But as these famous Olympians have shown, girls have the speed, stamina, and skill needed to play a fiercely competitive sport like ice hockey.

Cammi Granato's name is on the list of the top ten dominant women in world hockey. As team captain, she led the U.S. women to the first ever Olympic gold medal in women's hockey. In 1996, she was named the USA Women's Player of the Year. Today, Granato works for the Los Angeles Kings as a radio commentator. She's the only female broadcaster in the National Hockey League.

Cammi Granato

Karyn Bye

Karyn Bye knows how to bring her best game to the ice. In 1995 and 1998, she was named USA Hockey Women's Player of the Year. She is a five-time member of the U.S. Women's National Team, playing in 1992, 1994, 1995, 1996, and 1997. But even those accomplishments couldn't top the excitement of winning the gold in the 1998 Olympics. Karyn was so excited about taking home the gold that she didn't take her medal off for three days. She even slept with it on!

Krissy Wendell

At age 2, Krissy Wendell began skating. But her parents made her wait until age 5 to compete in hockey. Wendell joined the U.S. Women's National Team in 1998, at age 17. She graduated from high school in 2000, having finished her high school career scoring 219 goals in 52 games. Wendell went on to play at the University of Minnesota and at the 2002 Winter Olympics.

The youngest player ever named to the U.S. Women's National Team, Natalie Darwitz joined the squad in 1999 at age 15. In her high school hockey career, Darwitz scored 312 goals and was credited with 175 assists. At the 2002 Winter Olympics in Salt Lake City, Utah, Darwitz helped her team earn a silver medal, scoring a team-high of seven goals. Playing college hockey for the University of Minnesota, Darwitz worked her way to the top of the school's all-time points with 246 goals and 144 assists.

Natalie Darwitz

When you're skating fast across the ice, it almost feels as though you are flying. And there's no better feeling than when you make an assist or score a goal.

Hockey fosters teamwork, good sportsmanship, and lifetime friendships. What better investment in your future could you ask for?

GLOSSARY

assist (uh-SIST)—the pass of a puck that leads to a teammate scoring a goal

body check (BOD-ee CHEK)—to hit with the shoulder or hip to take an opponent out of play

elite (i-LEET)—a group of people who have special advantages or talents

face-off (FAYSS-OF)—a way to begin play where two players face each other and try to get control of the puck

league (LEEG)—a group of people with a common interest or activity, such as a sports team

opponent (uh-POH-nuhnt)—someone who is against you in a fight, contest, or game

penalty (PEN-uhl-tee)—a punishment for breaking the rules

FAST FACTS

 The most successful sports team in Canadian history is an all-women's ice hockey team. Between 1930 and 1940, the Preston Rivulettes played about 350 games and only lost two.

Manon Rheaume claims many firsts in women's hockey. In 1992, she became the first woman to play in an NHL game. She was also the first woman to sign a professional hockey contract and the first to play in a professional hockey game during the regular season.

READ MORE

Ditchfield, Christin. *Ice Hockey*. A True Book. New York.: Children's Press, 2003.

Kennedy, Mike. *Ice Hockey*. Watts Library. New York: F. Watts, 2003.

Thomas, Keltie. *How Hockey Works*. How Sports Work. Toronto, Ontario: Maple Tree Press, 2006.

INTERNET SITES

FactHound offers a safe, fun way to find Internet sites related to this book. All of the sites on FactHound have been researched by our staff.

Here's how:

1. Visit *www.facthound.com*

2. Choose your grade level.

3. Type in this book ID **1429601337** for age-appropriate sites. You may also browse subjects by clicking on letters, or by clicking on pictures and words.

4. Click on the **Fetch It** button.

Facthound will fetch the best sites for you!

ABOUT THE AUTHOR

Tami Johnson started out as an average hockey mom. She did fund-raising and produced a youth association hockey newsletter. Then she earned her coaching certificate and served as assistant coach for a girls' hockey team. At age 40, Johnson played her own first hockey game. After two years of playing goalie, she tried skating out and has played wing ever since.

INDEX